A Slave

To A

System

of

CRIME

JOSEPH WILTZ

A Slave to a System of Crime

Copyright © 2015 by Joseph Wiltz

Cover Design: TamikaInk.com

Edited by: Tamika Hall

ISBN-13: 9781515193517

DEDICATION

This book is dedicated to my wife Donna. Thank you for the faith that you have exemplified in me. I thank God for you. Without God and you, I do not know where I would be today. Your unconditional love and unending support has helped me to have the strength to be who I am today. I love you with a love that will last for eternity.

I also would like to acknowledge thank my best friend and cousin, Joseph Earl Lastrapes for playing a very important role in my life at an early age. I have learned so much about life and black history from him throughout the years.

ACKNOWLEDGEMENTS

I want to thank God for giving me the wisdom, knowledge, gifts, and talents that he has blessed me with. Without God I could not write this book. I also want to thank my lovely wife Donna for supporting me and being there for me spiritually. Our relationship with God caused us to have compassion for the people that have been hurt, as well as those who have hurt someone.

The facts in this book do not encourage racism, or agree with racism in any shape form or fashion. These facts are to hopefully help those who have been struggling for years to understand and find a solution to the horrible epidemic that has plagued the black race and black communities. I felt the need to uncover the truth that has been covered for much too long. God loves everyone and his desire is for all men to love one another and treat each other with justice and equality.

I also want to acknowledge the brothers in Prison that confided in me when employed as a prison guard. They shared some valuable and pertinent information with me which enabled me to have facts about the things that have caused many of them to continuously be a slave to the system. My heart goes out to the victims of crime and the perpetrator.

My prayer is that God will enlighten those who read this book, and hopefully fall into the hands of someone who truly cares and is in a position to bring about change that will set these brothers free from a mentality that has kept them captive far too long. Let truth be told, no one who is in authority really wants to bring peace in the black communities. It is just words being spoken to convince those who hear that they are concern.

Why has it been going on for so many years? When is it going to cease? When there are few black men left? If this was happening in the white communities, do you think that it would go this far.

It is time for us to stop hurting our people. Oh yes, we are hurting them every time we remain silent and refuse to address the truth due to fear and the need to maintain self-gratification.

For years the black race has been afraid to address race issues because they were afraid of what would happen to them. I watched prominent black men and women sit back and watch their race deteriorate from the face of the earth due to the oppression inflicted on those who were left alone to defend themselves without any weapons. When I speak of weapons, I am referring to mental and spiritual weapons.

Let's just lay aside our philosophy for a minute and conduct an evaluation on the amount of black men and women who do not have a high school education. How far do you think most of them will go in life? If for the sake of life we are not able to see that something is definitely wrong in America when the prisons are filled with predominately black males and females, black neighborhoods are filled with drugs, murder growing rampart, laws being pass that deprives a person with a felony from voting, then we too are victims of selfishness and ignorance.

If Martin Luther King would have said, "I am not going to put my life on the line for the uneducated or the simpletons, "Where would we be today? If Jesus Christ would have said, "I am not going to die on the cross for those wicked and sinful people," where would we be today? But we have the audacity to think that we are too educated and too prosperous to use the positions God placed us in to bring justice and equality!

TABLE OF CONTENTS

CHAPTER 1

THE REAL TRUTH ABOUT BLACK ON BLACK KILLINGS

We all know that when you sweep dirt under a rug, you can no longer see its appearance. This causes surface around the rug to appear clean. In other words, hiding the fact that there is a problem with cleanliness in the residence. When you place a bandage on a wound, you no longer see it making the skin appear to be ok. When someone wants a tree removed, the first and most appropriate thing to do is cut down the tree. Once the tree is cut you no longer see it. If it is cut all the way down to the ground, it is sometimes difficult to locate its existence. However, when the roots of the tree are dug up below the surface of the ground, the tree will be permanently removed and will not reappear.

When attempting to solve the epidemic of black on black crime or killings, we must first recognize the root of the problem and work on removing the root so that the same problem does not reoccur. How can one solve a problem that they have never experienced? We understand that the leaders in society attempt to make efforts to solve this horrible epidemic that has plagued the black race for years. We wish it would be as easy as saying, "We need to educate our young men and women so that they will have hope and be able to obtain jobs so that they would not have to live a life of poverty, sell drugs, sell their bodies, steal or get hooked on drugs."

It is vital that we have an understanding and first-hand experience of the things that cause our young black men and women to indulge in criminal behavior. Until we recognize the root of the problem and work on removing it we will only be putting a bandage on a cut without using the proper solution or medication to bring healing. If you have never been a black man, you do not understand how and why a black man thinks or feels the way he does.

There is a deviating matter that has gone undetected or should I say, intentionally undetected.

This matter deals with a broken system that has caused many black men and women to drop out of school because they were treated like they were to illiterate to learn by some educators. These same educators would not put much effort in tutoring them or spending extra time with them in an effort to encourage them and let them know that they can do whatever they set their minds to. Those who had parents who were not involved in their education were more likely to lose interest. When some educators realized that certain parents were not actively involved in their children's education, they would not show any interest either.

Until we get to the point where we start realizing that race issue's led to the horrific situation we are faced with today regarding poverty, the selling of drugs, and uncontrollable murders within the black race, we will forever have trouble finding solutions to the problem. For years, people have sugarcoated and covered the issue of race in America, which has led to one-third or more young black men and women being uneducated and feeling worthless.

Once they accept that lie, it begins to lead them into a life of total destruction. Some may say that this is a misconception because there are alot of educated blacks with good jobs who are living productive lives. That would not be an understatement; however, the statistics of black men and women who are uneducated and or incarcerated speaks for itself.

The average black person who is incarcerated is uneducated. The average black woman who is on welfare and food stamps is uneducated. What type of mentality and behavior would that person execute? Many blacks who have succeeded in life claim that the situation some of our black men and women face is their fault, and that they use excuses for their actions. I must admit that to a degree this is partially true.

We must again understand that not everyone is as strong as others, and everyone is not as fortunate as others. We must look at this with an open mind. No problem is solved without understanding. This problem is so deep and broad, that only spiritual wisdom and spiritual understanding will reveal the truth about it.

One may ask, "What does spiritual wisdom and understanding have to do with solving problems?" Well, I'll tell you, spiritual things come from God, and He is perfect. When God reveals something to someone, it is coming from the only perfect being in the world. God's revelation is not mixed with assumptions or knowledge that came from another imperfect being.

I am sure by now that if man alone could have solved this problem, we would not be experiencing the continuous climb of black on black crime and the urgency of law governing bodies to obtain a speedy resolution.Let's start with the root of the problems:

LACK OF EDUCATION:

If we were to do research, we would find that many of the young black men and black women who drop out of school come out of homes where either the father, mother, or both, may not have a high school education, resulting in the parent(s) working low paying jobs.

If the man of the house has a number of children, it may result in him having to obtain more than one job. This means that the father spends most of his time working, and less time at home raising the children. The frustration of the father having to work so much and come home to children who are screaming and shouting, on occasion causes the father to want to find a way of escape, or a way to ease his mind. Therefore, he drinks alcohol, clubs, or even uses drugs, thinking that this will help him through the tough times. The frustration

A SLAVE TO A SYSTEM OF CRIME

sometimes causes men to be unloving to their wives, hostile, and violent.

When violence enters the home, we now have a situation where the children are experiencing frustration, anger, oppression, depression, verbal abuse, and even physical abuse in the home. Some even experience their fathers having extra-marital affairs. How can this type of behavior not effect children's perception about life. On many occasions some children go to school wearing horrible clothing, busted shoes, and get teased by other children. When there are functions or some kind of activities at the school that require money to enter, the less fortunate children are not able to attend. This brings about embarrassment and add on to the issues at home.

Let's not forget those who grow up without a father and the mother has to work to provide for the children. If the mother does not have a high school education, she has to accept minimum wage jobs. Can you imagine what that mother has to go through if she has more than one or two children to provide for? When that mother gets home, her day is not over. She has to make sure that the children have food to eat and clothing to wear. The mother, if not strong like the man mentioned above, will experience hopelessness, frustration and depression; sometimes causing her to become desperate for companionship and make emotional decisions. She may be lucky and find the right man, or she may find the wrong man and make her life and her children's life worst, leading to destructive life experiences.

We can see here how a lack of education can cause a chain of destructive attitudes and behavior. These attitudes and behavior, if not recognized, understood, and corrected, can lead to permanent destruction in their lives and the lives of other innocent people.

CHAPTER 2

A PARENT'S EFFECT ON CHILDREN DUE TO LACK OF EDUCATION

Now that all of these negative traits have been deposited into the mind and spirit of the children, they begin implementing what they have experienced. They do not have any education; therefore, most of them experience poverty at an early stage in their lives and begin to do things that they think would give them a sense of worth. How many of us know that a depressed and oppressed person has abnormal ways of thinking.

Poverty is a disease that effects the brain and causes abnormal functioning. In all essence, it eventually begins to affect every part of the body, and cause some to become alcoholics, drug addicts, prostitutes, murderers, thieves, etc.

On most occasions, they will do whatever it takes to survive or feel a sense of financial security. Once these debilitating traits evolve, crime begins. Some believe that selling drugs is the best way out. The selling of drugs lead to a more destructive lifestyle. Now there are weapons involved. The need to be validated and recognized becomes a desperate need, so here comes the ride with the 22's or 24's, then the boom box, and the name brand clothes and shoes. Once these things have been accomplished, here comes the young ladies.

Feeling important and special in their own minds, they begin to feel that they deserve the utmost respect, still mentally disturbed and confused from the upbringing, they start mistreating the young ladies, verbally, mentally, and physically. The young women end up getting pregnant, having children, only to be raised in the same environment.

Eventually the spirit of competition kicks in, and the young men want to outdo one another.

There goes the all-out war for power or recognition that they never received while in school or growing up. Then the killing begins because someone that sold drugs for them messed them over, or someone is on their turf, or trying to get with their lady. Then there are those who are robbing others to get what they want. The black neighborhoods become infested with drug dealers on every corner, gun shots ringing through the streets, and no one knows what happened. Eventually someone comes forward to witness the crime, and that person turns up dead. This is a cycle that must be broken. This is called, "learned behavior," young men telling their little boys not to take anything from anyone at an early age, corrupting them through their lifestyles. This lifestyle leads our young to prison; most of them before the age of 18 or 20.

THE NEGATIVE EFFECTS OF PRISON:

Most people think that if they go to prison, they will change their lives and become better people in society. That is not a fact. In fact, the majority of people that go to prison become more corrupt than they were before they went there. You would think that prison would be a place where people would go and be rehabilitated, but that is not so. It is just what it says it is - a place of harsh punishment. From my working in the prison system, I had first-hand experience with the corruption and the mental destruction that exists in these places.

I once observed an 18 year old black male enter the prison system for allegedly carrying a machete knife that he found on the side of the street while walking from New Orleans to Baton Rouge, in order to find employment. This was this young man's first time being arrested. He was placed in a cell block with other inmates that had been in and out of prison. The young man could not adjust to this and it began to drive him crazy. He started sleeping under his bunk over wet pieces of tissue paper that he placed under the bunk. He was fearful.

A couple of the inmates that were accustomed the system, would jam their cell doors and come out of their cells when the officers were not around. One of the inmates began to offer the young man cigarettes, food, and other items he thought the young man needed. One would have thought that he was doing this as an act of kindness. However, he was doing this in order to have control of the young man so that he could perform a sex act with him. The young man had no idea that he was being set up because he had never been in a situation like that before.

One morning when the young man was let out of his cell to take a shower, the older inmate exited his cell and cornered the young man in the shower and proceeded to penetrate him in the rectum with his finger. The young man screamed for the guards and banged on the iron door until someone responded nearly 10 minutes later. This was enough time for the young man to be raped and possibly killed. When they did respond, the older inmate had returned to his cell, and stated that the young man was lying.

The young man was removed from his cell and placed in another that was worse. If this young man becomes violent and starts hurting other people, it will be said that he is a problem, and that he has been incarcerated before. Some would say he never learned a lesson. No wonder when most young men go to jail for the first time, they become corrupt and on most occasions end up going back. So many have been forced to get used to a system that instills more hatred and violence in them than they had before going there.

So often guards leave inmates unattended, and people wonder how someone can be raped or murdered. According to the department of Justice, more men are raped in prisons in the U.S. than women. In 2008 it was estimated that 216,000 inmates were assaulted in detention. In 2011, 4 percent of prisoners said that they had been sexually abused.

I have witnessed a guard let an inmate out of his cell and opened the cell of another inmate in order for this inmate to beat the other inmate. He started hitting the inmate until the inmate was full of blood. When the inmate looked up and saw the guard standing on the tier, he ran to the guard for help, and when he got close to the guard, the guard punched him in the stomach and he fell onto the floor. The guard started kicking the inmate in the head and in the stomach. Shortly after, the guard told the inmate that he was taking him to see the doctor, and that he better not mention what happened. He told him to say something else.

I have also witnessed guards bringing drugs into the prison and giving it to the inmates, and an outside friend or family member of the inmate would pay the guard. If we do research, we will discover that the majority of murders committed, have been committed by someone that has been incarcerated before. So what makes one think that the problem with black on black killings will be solved only by educating our young men?

Yes, I agree that education is a very important factor, but for those who already have a destructive mentality and have been institutionalized, it is evident that there are other deep rooted issues that need to be acknowledged and understood. Exploring these issues will help correct this long hidden fact of corruption and destruction.

You may ask "Why do the Wardens not know that these things are going on?" In some cases, the Wardens and Sheriffs don't know because the guards do not let this type of information get to them. The Wardens and or Sheriffs do not spend lots of time in the dormitories and cell blocks in order to monitor what's going on. Yes we know that they should have cameras in every area of the prisons, but unfortunately, not every area have cameras.

I have a brother who was arrested for a traffic violation in the state of Texas and the officers were interrogating him violently. He became upset and told them he was not answering anymore questions so they attacked him, threw him onto the floor on his stomach with his hands cuffed in the back, and proceeded to beat him, choke him, and attempted to pull his eyeball out. The following day, I arrived at the Sheriff's office and met with the Sheriff.

The Sheriff advised that he did not know anything about this. I showed him some pictures of my brother's face looking deformed and he was shocked. I informed the NAACP and we set up an appointment with the Sheriff to discuss this serious problem. It was then reported to the news media and aired on CNN. Through our meetings with the Sheriff of that county, we learned that this officer had numerous complaints against him over the years for the same matter and they did not release him from his duties. After this incident, they had no other choice but to release him and charges were brought against him.

So often our young black men are abused by other inmates or officers and nothing is done because once they go to prison they are no longer looked at as a human beings. They are viewed as animals having to defend themselves by any means necessary. The means are normally violence. This type of behavior becomes normal to them, so when they are released from prison, most of them remain in the same state of mind, and continue with the same behavior.

There is no rehabilitation program in place that helps prepare these men morally, mentally, or spiritually, when they exit the prison system and are released into the free world. Whenever one's mind has been forcefully transformed or traumatized, it is very important for that person to obtain some form of rehabilitation. When the soldiers are preparing to depart from war and return to their families or homes, the government will do all that they must do to help prepare them mentally for the transition because they know how important this is to the future of the soldiers, their families, and society.

Some may say that there is no comparison because these people have committed crimes. Although they may have committed crimes, if they did the time and the system is allowing them back into society, then they to need to be prepared for a life that is different from the traumatic environment they were in. If it's important to help them not re-offend and go back to prison, then there must be a system in place to accommodate.

I personally believe that for the men that will be back out on the streets someday, there should be mental evaluations conducted on them to determine what areas of counseling they will need. I also think that it would be a good idea to put some kind of monitoring system in place, so that the law-makers are able to see what is really going on with the prison system. I believe this is essential if they want to help find a solution to the horrific epidemic of black on black killings.

THE JUSTICE SYSTEM:

It is time that we take a closer look at our justice system. When I was a police officer, I had first-hand experience with police officers who charged people with charges that did not fit the crime or relevant to the crime. Some of them will intentionally add as many charges as they possibly can so that they can make a case. Even if there was a plea bargain offered, most of the time, the person was forced to still plead to a felony. Whereas, if the charge would be only for the crime committed, there is a possibility that a person would be charged with a lesser charge under a plea bargain.

It is so ironic that majority of the times, unless the crime is a simple traffic violation, a person ends up with a felony charge. We understand that there is a sense of loyalty and trust between the courts and police officers, but it does not help those who are wrongly accused of committing crimes and have to suffer the consequences of having their freedom taken away.

It continues on after one is released; then comes the problem of not being able to find a job because of the felony record. I am not saying that everyone with a felony record cannot find jobs, because there are people with felony records in the workforce. What I am saying is on the average, it is more difficult to find employment with a felony record.

We know that not hiring someone due to the fact that they have a felony record could constitute discrimination, so that is why no one will be told that they cannot be hired because of their record, unless it conflicts with the duties of the position. In most cases, people are told that the position has been filled, or there is no opening. I also believe that there should be an organization in place to monitor how many convicted felons are employed, how many are not employed and then allow them the opportunity to discuss their problems or frustrations in obtaining employment. This is another serious issue when we talk about repeat offenders.

If a person is constantly being turned down everywhere they go for employment, it eventually frustrates them to the point that they become hopeless and want to do the next best thing to survive. By no means are we not aware that there are some that just don't want to be gainfully employed, but we are speaking about those who still have hope and want to change, those who want to make a difference. So often we hear those who have never experienced anything like this say, "People find excuses for everything."

I must agree that there are some that look for excuses, but we cannot judge everyone alike. It would be like saying that you are just like your co-worker or best friend who steals from the government or defrauds the system. If there is going to be an effort to solve the epidemic of black on black killings, we must look at the entire picture and must not be bias or go in with a negative mind.

CHAPTER 3

SEXUAL MISCONDUCT IN PRISONS

The Human Rights Watch reported statistics compiled by the U.S. Justice Department agency. The statistics revealed that the rape and sexual abuse of prisoners by other prisoners and staff plague prisons nationwide. According to the **Sexual victimization in state and Federal prisons reported by inmates Report** released by the Bureau of Justice statistics in 2007:

4.5 percent of the state and federal prisoners surveyed reported sexual victimization in the past 12 months. Given a national prison population of 1,570,861, the Bureau of Justice statistics suggest that in one year alone more than 70,000 prisoners were sexually abused.

When one in 20 prisoners report being raped or sexually abused behind bars, it is clear that prison authorities are not doing enough to prevent these serious crimes. Prison rape is not inevitable, but it is all too predictable when prison authorities fail to enforce a zero- tolerance policy on sexual abuse.

Some 2.1 percent of inmates surveyed by the Bureau of Justice statistics reported sexual abuse involving another inmate. In its 2001 landmark report, male rape in U.S. prisons, Human Rights Watch documented vicious and brutally violent male rapes in prison as well as other more common, less overtly violent forms of coerced sex. Certain prisoners are more vulnerable to rape and are targeted for sexual exploitation- especially prisoners who are young, physically small or weak, gay, first offenders or have been convicted of a sexual offense against a minor or women.

Sexual abuse by other inmates often occurs because staff fail to adequately supervise inmates or respond appropriately to complaints of unwanted sexual activity. In some prisons, staff tacitly as well as explicitly condoned inmate – on-inmate abuse. Nationwide, a higher percentage of inmates, 2.9 percent, reported staff sexual misconduct than inmate-on-inmate abuse.

Through conversations with people who have been incarcerated for decades, I learned that when guards do not like a particular inmate, they will set that inmate up to get raped or killed by other inmates. The guards would wait until everyone were asleep, slowly open the target inmates cell whereas he was unable to hear the door open, and allow the another inmate to enter the cell, stab the inmate to death and leave the area without anyone knowing other than the guard and the killer. The guard would then cover up all of the evidence, and no further actions would be taken in the matter. The guard would fabricate a story to tell the inmates family.

THE EFFECTS OF PRISON RAPE

Prison rape is extremely detrimental to the mental and psychological state of a human being. The raped inmate eventually becomes bitter, angry, and psychologically dysfunctional. That person's behavior at some point becomes destructive, whereas that inmate's mindset is now focused on revenge on anyone who gets in his way or he deems to be attacked as he was.

In most cases, some inmates begin raping other vulnerable or first offense inmates. In doing such, that inmate will physically and violently attack the person he is pursuing because that is what he learned from what happened to him. Due to the mental trauma inflicted on the raped inmates, most of them become extremely violent and in some cases end up killing someone.

The mental state of these raped inmates becomes totally transformed into the mental state of an animal, feeling that the only way to survive in prison is to have and maintain a, "No feeling, No conscience mentality." Since they were not protected by the guards, they don't depend on the guards and they begin to acquire weapons through sources in the prison to use for their attacks on others as well as their protection.

I am quite sure that you would agree that the effects a man experiences from something so traumatic and degrading will have a lasting negative effect on him. Take a moment and ask yourself these questions:

- What type of counseling or psychiatric help is given to these inmates when they are eligible for release?
- What type of behavior will these inmates illustrate in the communities in which they are going back too?
- How about the inmates who have not reported being raped because of embarrassment and will not receive any

counseling because there were no records of the incident?

I can assure you that this type of abnormal treatment will never be cured through any man. The reason is because there are evil and satanic forces that have come against the very existence of the God created mind, soul, and spirit. Therefore, it is only through the supernatural powers of God, that man can be totally healed from such wicked and evil trauma.

CHAPTER 4

SOLITARY CONFINEMENT: THE WORST KIND OF PSYCHOLOGICAL TORTURE

Though the impact of solitary confinement differs from person to person, there are some basic symptoms. There may be as much as 80,000 American prisoners locked up in segregation housing units. Solitary confinement in a segregated housing unit can cause irreversible psychological effects in as little as 15 days. Here's what social isolation does to your brain, and why it should be considered torture.

There's no universal definition for solitary confinement, but the United Nations describes it as any regime where an inmate is held in isolation from others, except guards for at least 23 hours a day.

Some jurisdictions allow prisoners out of their cells for one hour of solitary exercise each day. But meaningful contact with others is typically reduced to a bare minimum. Prisoners are also intentionally deprived of stimulus; available stimuli and fleeting rare social contacts are rarely chosen by the prisoners, and are typically monotonous and inconsiderate of their needs.

Human beings are social creatures. Without the benefit of another person to, "bounce off of," the Mind decays. Without anything to do, the brain atrophies; and without the ability to see off in the distance, vision fades. Isolation and loss of control breeds anger, anxiety, and hopelessness. Psychologist Terry Kupers says that solitary confinement, "Destroys people as human beings."
Here are some of the symptoms:

- Depression: Emotional flatness/blunting and loss of ability to have any "feelings", mood swings, hopelessness, Social withdraws, loss of initiation, of activity, or ideas, apathy, lethargy, major depression

- **Anxiety:** Persistent low level of stress , irritability, anxiousness, panic attacks, fear of impending death.

- **Paranoia:** Recurrent and persistent thoughts, often of a violent and vengeful character (e.g. directed against (Prison staff) paranoid ideas (often persecutory), psychotic episodes or states, psychotic depression and Schizophrenia.

- **Anger:** Irritability and hostility, poor impulse control, outburst of physical and verbal violence against others, self, and objects, unprovoked angers, sometimes manifested as rage.

- **Perceptual distortions:** Hypersensitivity to noises and smell, distortions of sensation (e.g. walls closing in), disorientation in time and space, depersonalization/de-realization, hallucinations affecting all five senses (e.g.

hallucination of objects or people appearing in the cell, or hearing voices when no one is speaking.

- **Cognitive disturbances:** Short attention span, poor concentration, and memory, confused thought process, Disorientation.

- **Self-harm:** Self-mutilation and cutting, suicide attempts

In terms of prevalence, somewhere between 8% and 19% of American prisoners will experience significant psychiatric or functional disabilities, while another 15% to 20% will require some form of psychiatric intervention during their incarceration.

The American Psychiatric Association says that up to 20% of all prisoners are, "Seriously mentally ill," whereas up to 5% are, "actively psychotic at any given moment. About 4% of inmates have schizophrenia or some other psychotic disorder, nearly 19% suffer from depression, and around 4% have bipolar disorder.

All who suffer from psychological torture of solitary confinement are placed on medication to help control or curb these emotions. However, there can never be medication to totally cure or restore them to their original mental state. They now have to depend on the medication to help manage their conditions forever, unless they encounter a divine intervention with God, the creator of the mind.

CHAPTER 5

NEGATIVE EFFECTS OF THE ABSENT PARENT ON THE CHILDREN

I have had first-hand experience with the absent parent syndrome by watching my own nieces and nephews become totally angry and uncontrollable after my brother left his wife with nine children to care for without a job. He departed and the anger of their mother escalated to where she did not want them to be around him. They became very angry and bitter because their father left them and their mother did not want them to spend time with their father. The constant arguments between he and his wife led to hatred.

My brother was unemployed at the time and could not provide for his children. Their mother obtained a job, but she was only able to make minimum wages due to the fact that she only had a

42 | P a g e

GED. This led to them having to be on welfare and food stamps. The children began having problems at school and in the neighborhood from other children who would tease them about their clothing and their hair. Most of the time they could not get hair-cuts or the girls could not get their hair done when needed.

This horrible upbringing caused the children to start getting in trouble at school. They were getting into fights with the students and the teachers. Their behavior eventually led to six of them being sent to behavior homes for youth. Once they were released, most of them ended up living with strangers. Some of them lived with single mothers who had children that were also involved in criminal activities. This did not help the problem. They got progressively worse and then their father wanted to have custody of them, but was still in no position to have custody because he was still unemployed and involved in excessive use of alcohol. They had no respect for him and they felt that he was at fault for what they were going through.

Eventually, one of them became involved with the wrong company and ended up in prison on an armed robbery charge at the age of 17. After being released from prison, he was having a very difficult time finding a job. He believed that it was because of his criminal record, so he became frustrated, lost hope, and began to follow bad company again.

There are still four children active in school at present and seem to be doing ok. One of my brothers and I wanted to take some of them in and help them, but they did not want to live with either one of us because they had problems with the fact that they would have to follow rules and regulations. They were used to having their way and did not want anyone telling them what to do.

At present, we have family gatherings, and they are there enjoying the love that we have for each other. The two oldest have been gainfully employed for years now, and the second daughter is graduating shortly. I thank God that my brothers and I maintained contact with them, and continued to show them love. I believe that the love we showed made a tremendous difference. When they call for a need, we do our best to be there for them. This is another reason why we must understand the root of a problem in order to effectively find a solution. It is so much easier for someone to say that this is not a reason for negative behavior or hopelessness; however, if you have never experienced a life like this you would not know.

I recall working in one of the penitentiaries here in Louisiana and talking to numerous inmates who stated that the bitterness and anger they had came from the fact that their fathers were not active in their lives. Some of them said that when they would see their friends with their fathers, and they could not enjoy such, it would make them angry and they would do things to get in trouble. Some inmates would tell me that they were so tired of seeing their mothers beaten by their boyfriends (and their mothers would not want to discontinue the relationship), they would become angry and look for some trouble to get into. I also had some tell me that because their fathers were not in their lives and their mothers could not give them the things they needed, they started living a life of crime, by selling drugs to make it, or committing robbery.

We cannot conclude that everyone who commits a crime wants to do this. Yes, I believe that after someone has been in prison for years, or half of their lives, they should want to change. I will say again, we must get to the root of the problem. Once someone has been in prison for a certain amount of time, they become institutionalized and therefore, will need some serious counseling in order to help them adjust to society.

CHAPTER 6

Police Tactics That Lead To False Confessions

The California Innocence Project uncovered that false confessions are one of the leading causes of wrongful convictions. False confession cases always result from the way that an interrogation has taken place. One of the most common interrogation techniques used by law enforcement officers, is the "Reid Technique." Officers are trained to first ask non-accusatory questions in order to determine if the subject is lying about their involvement in a crime. If the officer believes the subject is lying, than an accusatory interrogation takes place. At this point the officer believes the subject is guilty, and the goal is to have the subject admit guilt.

Factors leading to wrongful Convictions:

- The cognitive biases of police investigation
- Unreliable scientific evidence, such as polygraph

- Hypnosis
- Poor lab work
- Coerced false confession
- Inaccurate eyewitness identification
- False accusations and perjured testimony
- Incompetent defense attorney

Most people who are arrested are De Facto guilty of something. This presumption of guilt, when it replaces the De Jure presumption of innocence, leads to wrongful convictions.

Studies show that an estimated 10,000 innocent people are convicted each year in the United States. Ronald Huff, director of Criminal Justice Research Center, created a database of 205 wrongful convictions collected from a variety of sources. After analyzing these cases, the researchers found that most wrongful convictions resulted from a combination of errors. The main cause in more than half of the cases, 52.3 percent was eyewitness misidentification.

The second reason was perjury by a witness, which contributed to 11 percent of the convictions. Other problems included negligence by Criminal Justice Officials, coerced confessions, "frame ups" by guilty parties, and general overzealousness by officers and prosecutors.

Although one may think most errors are unintentional, research shows that there are far too many incidents of unethical and unprofessional behavior.

CHAPTER 7

STATISTICS OF BLACKS INCARCERATED IN THE U.S. vs. WHITES

According to the NAACP, a report dated August 2013, reported on racial disparities in the United States, and stated that African Americans constitute nearly one million of the total 2.3 million incarcerated population. This is nearly six times the rate of whites. In 2009 the percentage of adult males incarcerated by race were:

- Hispanics: 1.8%
- Blacks: 4.7%
- Whites: 0.7%
- All: 1.4%

The report states that there are more black men under correctional control today than there were in slavery in 1850.

According to the Pew Research Center, black men were more than six times as likely as white men in 2010 to be incarcerated in federal and state prisons, and local jails. In 2010, the incarceration rate for white men under local, state and federal jurisdiction was 678 inmates per 100,000 white U.S. residents; for black men, it was 4,347. The Bureau of Justice Statistics revealed that black men were more than six times as likely as white men to be incarcerated in 2010.

Fifty years after Lyndon B. Johnson signed the 1964 civil rights act into Law there still remains gaps between blacks and whites on many social and economic measures. A Pew Research Center study in 2013 stated the black, white gaps in median household income and wealth had widened in recent decades.

CHAPTER 8

IS THE PLEA BARGAIN A BENEFIT TO BLACK AMERICANS?

Plea bargain in the United States is very common; the vast majority of criminal cases in the United States are settled by plea bargain rather than by a jury trial. The constitutionality of plea bargain was established by Brady vs. United States in 1970. Although the Supreme Court warned that plea incentives that were sufficiently large or coercive as to over-rule defendant's ability to act freely, or used in a manner giving rise to a significant number of innocent people pleading guilty, might be prohibited or lead to concerns over constitutionality.

Several features of the American Justice System tend to promote plea bargaining. The adversarial nature of the system puts judges in a passive role, in which they are completely dependent upon the parties to develop the factual record and cannot independently discover information with which to assess the strength of the case against the defendant. The parties thus can control the outcome of the case by exercising their rights or bargaining them away.

For a plea to be valid, it must meet the following conditions:

- Defendant must be, "Fully aware of the direct consequences, including the actual value of any commitments made to him."

- Plea must be, "Induced by threats (or promises to discontinue improper harassment), misrepresentation (including unfulfilled or unfulfillable promises), or perhaps by promises that are by their nature improper as having no proper relationship to the prosecutor's business (e.g. bribes)."

Pleas entered would not become invalid later merely due to a wish to reconsider the judgment which led to them, or better information about the defendant's or the state's case, or the legal position.

Plea bargaining is no more foolproof than full trials to the court or to the jury. There would be serious doubt about a case if the encouragement of guilty pleas by offers of leniency substantially increased the likelihood that defendant's advised by competent counsel, would falsely condemn themselves. This view is to the contrary and is based on expectations that courts will satisfy themselves that pleas of guilt are voluntarily and intelligently made by competent defendants with adequate advice of counsel and that there is nothing to question the accuracy and reliability of the defendant's admissions.

Even when the charges are more serious, prosecutors can often bluff the defense attorney and their clients into pleading guilty to a lesser charge.

CHAPTER 9

IDENTIFYING PROSECUTORIAL MISCONDUCT

Prosecutorial misconduct is, "An illegal act or failing to act, on the part of a prosecutor, especially an attempt to sway the Jury to wrongly convict a defendant or to impose a harsher than appropriate punishment." It is similar to selective prosecution.

Types of Misconduct:

- False Confession
- Falsified evidence
- Intimidation
- Police brutality-abetting
- Prosecutorial corruption
- Political repression
- Racial profiling
- Sexual abuse
- Surveillance abuse-abetting
- Testifying-subornation of perjury

- Failure to disclose exculpatory evidence

Abuse of Discretion:

- Selective prosecution by race, income, political affiliation, etc.

- Capture of the grand jury, misusing it as tool for inquisitorial abuse, or excluding citizen's complaints from being heard.

- Plea bargaining abuses, such as seeking testimony in exchange for leniency, this may solicit perjury or falsified evidence.

- Threatening public officials, especially Judges with prosecution if they don't unduly support their cases

- Tainting of Jury pools with public statements by prosecutors that are either, inaccurate, exaggerated, unsupported by evidence or that could be inadmissible at trial, and such statements become widely promulgated by the media

- Prosecutors using multi-defendant trials to get defendants to turn on one another in the courtroom, as Judges may be reluctant to allow separate trials in multi- defendant cases.

The Los Angeles times noted on January 31, 2015, that 9th circuit court Alex Kozinski and two other Judges expressed their frustration over the fact that the California State Judges were not cracking down on prosecutorial misconduct. Kozinski stated that prosecutors are going to continue committing prosecutorial misconduct because of State Judges looking the other way.

Research shows that prosecutorial misconduct is not being committed only in California, but prosecutorial misconduct is wide spread, and has become an epidemic across America. It is the duty of State court Judges to crack down on prosecutorial misconduct. However, it is not being done. This makes the Judges just as responsible for that type of conduct by allowing it to go on.

I can honestly attest to what Judge Kozinski stated, according to my personal experience with prosecutorial misconduct. I was conspired upon by two prosecutors in an attempt to force me into a plea bargain concerning a felony theft charge in which the police fabricated. The charges were dismissed. One of the prosecutors handling the probation revocation matter in which I was on probation, at the time of the felony theft charge, called the other prosecutor, who was no longer handling the felony theft charge, and coerced him into filing a re-indictment.

The prosecutor handling the probation revocation told my attorney that she wanted me to accept a plea bargain of a lesser charge than felony theft, and they would reduce it to a misdemeanor and I would spend one year in Jail. I told my attorney that I was not going to let them coerce me like they did the first time. I was already aware of the fact that the prosecutor handling the revocation had a vendetta against me due to the fact that I attempted to get an early probation release since I had never been arrested or convicted before.

The prosecutor became upset and thought that I was challenging her authority. She also mentioned it to my attorney and her friend. The Attorney I had at the time had close relations with her and every time my Attorney and I meet, he would tell me that she had it in for me.

Once I realized that my Attorney was intentionally incompetent, due to his untruthfulness, and deception, I immediately terminated him and hired another. The new attorney consulted with the prosecutor handling the felony theft charge and she dismissed the charges.

Approximately one month after the charges were re-instituted I had to hire my third attorney. My third attorney immediately filed a motion to quash and dismiss according to the expiration of the statute of limitations. At this time seven years had passed and we were still dealing with this matter. When my Attorney and I appeared in court on the motion, the initial prosecutor who was conspiring with the prosecutor handling the revocation appeared in court. He argued that he was in court the morning that the case was dismissed, but he left the court room. He also stated that he did not make any arrangements with my first attorney to dismiss the matter once restitution was paid, he stated that my first attorney whom I had already terminated was standing by to testify and that he and the co-defendant's attorney spoke in court that morning and decided to set the co-defendant for status, and set mine for trial. He then stated that the prosecutor who dismissed the charges did not have the authority to do so but he was moved to another court, and therefore, the case was assigned to the prosecutor who dismissed it. Therefore, the Judge denied the motion and proceeded to set my case for trial.

I informed my third attorney, that the prosecutor lied in court under oath because he was not in court that morning, nor was the codefendants Attorney that he claim to have conversed with. My attorney requested the court transcripts from the date of the dismissal, and the date of the motion hearing. Upon receipt of the transcripts, my attorney reviewed all documents, and concluded that the prosecutor did in fact lie in court, which constitutes prosecutorial misconduct, alone with him conspiring with the prosecutor handling the revocation, in an effort to coerce me into a plea bargain.

My attorney immediately filed another motion to reconsider, as well as the evidence of the prosecutor's misconduct. At this time, I filed a complaint against this prosecutor with the attorney Disciplinary Board. Prior to the court date, I received a letter from the disciplinary board, advising that the complaint was premature, and that they would keep the complaint on file. They also stated that should any new information come up after we go to court, please let them know.

Approximately one month after, I had a court appearance in another court for the revocation hearing. The prosecutor that had the vendetta against me was not handling the matter after seven years of handling it. The prosecutor, whom she had to file the re-indictment was now handling the matter. For the revocation hearing He subpoenaed witnesses or alleged witnesses of the felony theft charge. He was attempting to make a trial out of it.

My Attorney informed the Judge that I (HER CLIENT) have a complaint filed against this particular prosecutor. The prosecutor stated to the Judge, that this was speculations, and my Attorney then approached the bench, and provided the certified copy of the complaint to the Judge. The Judge then called for recess and called my attorney and the prosecutor to the back. When they re-entered the court room, the Judge rescheduled the revocation hearing per request of the prosecutor and agreement of my attorney.

Prior to our next court date for the felony theft charge, my Attorney was informed by the prosecutor who committed misconduct that the head District Attorney wanted to speak to her. She accepted the request. He stated to her that the NAACP contacted him in reference to a complaint that her client filed against one of his assistants, and that they are not worried about it and their position is still the same.

A person who is an Attorney and chairman of the black caucus contacted the head D.A. and advised him that she had the opportunity to review all the documents pertaining to this matter. Based on her findings she suggested that the matter be dismissed before it turned into a media frenzy and the administration be forced to fire him. However, when the co-defendant and I appeared in court for the motion, the initial prosecutor that re-indicted us dismissed the case.

Four months after dismissing the felony theft charge, the same prosecutor who filed the re-indictment informed my ttorney that they were not going to pursue the probation revocation and that it would be dismissed. However, it wasn't until we appeared in court that I found out that the revocation was being terminated unsatisfactorily. The Judge stated that because of the arrest, which happened eight years earlier, he would have to terminate it unsatisfactorily , although he stated that I was in compliance the entire 10 years I was on probation.

I was initially on probation for a five year period, however, the fabricated felony theft charge extended my probation an additional five years. I share my story to truly let you know that I am very aware of the epidemic of prosecutorial misconduct because I experienced it firsthand. Truth be told, we are supposed to be afraid to expose the truth about injustice, and those in power, who abuse and misuse their authority, because of fear of retaliation.

According to the disparities of blacks and whites incarcerated in America, the evidence proves that judges as well as prosecutors are responsible for the injustice inflicted on Blacks in America.

Sometimes, prosecutors find evidence that would exonerate the person they are trying to convict, but because prosecutors are charged with representing the truth, the prosecution is obligated to turn over exculpatory evidence. Many legal scholars, prosecutorial misconduct has been seriously underreported. John G. Browning of the Albany Law School stated that one study using a computer- assisted review revealed that there have only been just over one hundred reported cases of professional discipline of Federal and State prosecutors in the past century. An average of approximately one disciplinary per year.

Why is that? Many reasons emerge, not the least of which is a practical, empirical obstacle to accurately assessing the problem: Prosecutors who engage in such misconduct presumably don't want to be caught, and will take steps to conceal their actions. Another reason is the autonomy enjoyed by prosecutor's offices insofar as their internal policies are concerned. The considerable discretion afforded to prosecutors over whom to prosecute and which offenses to charge, coupled with a lack of external oversight of prosecutors offices, foster's an environment in which misconduct can remain undetected and unchecked. Yet another reason is sheer volume. Most criminal cases in the United States result in plea bargain, which are rarely subjected to judicial review or extensive investigation. Consequently, the vast majority of known examples of prosecutorial misconduct only came to light during long, drawn out trials or over the course of an appeal.

Chapter 10

EPIDEMIC OF PROSECUTORIAL MISCONDUCT

The prosecutor has more control over life, liberty, and reputation than any other person in America. His discretion is tremendous. While the prosecutor at his best is one of the most beneficent forces in our society, when he acts from malice or other base motives, he is one of the worst. – Former U.S. Attorney

When persons envision the wheels of justice in motion, they picture a black-robed judge solemnly presiding over a prosecutor, defense attorney, defendant, and impassive members of the jury. Such a depiction may have been true a generation ago. But now the great majority of convictions are reached by means of a prosecutor-negotiated plea bargain—representing over 90% of all criminal cases. Prosecutors make fateful decisions about whether to order an arrest, disclose evidence to the defense, propose the terms of a plea bargain, and make sentencing recommendations to the judge. Most important, prosecutors decide whom to charge and what crimes to charge them with.

District attorneys are called upon to play a dual role, serving both as advocates for victims as well as ministers of justice. The U.S. Supreme Court has explained:

Society wins not only when the guilty are convicted but when criminal trials are fair; our system of the administration of justice suffers when any accused is treated unfairly.

The overwhelming majority of lawyers who choose to become prosecutors are ethical. But powerful incentives – political ambitions, media pressures, and a culture of prosecutorial infallibility – can serve to induce prosecutors to act unethically.

68 | P a g e

This White Paper explores the question, "How well are American prosecutors discharging their oath-bound duty to act as ministers of justice?"

FALL OF WRONGFUL CONVICTIONS

"Innocent men are never convicted. Don't worry about it, it never happens in the world. It is a physical impossibility."

Wrongful convictions were once presumed to be extremely rare, even non-existent in our criminal justice system, as this quotation reveals. But the advent of DNA analysis in the late 1980s opened up the possibility of post-conviction DNA testing, often serving to exclude the person convicted of the crime. To date, over 1,200 persons have been exonerated following DNA analysis, witness recantation, confession by the actual offender, or by other means.

Estimates of the extent of wrongful convictions vary. A 2007 analysis of persons sentenced to death from 1973 to 2004 yielded a 2.3% exoneration rate. A more recent study of post-conviction DNA analyses in Virginia found that for 15% of persons convicted of sexual assault, the defendant was later excluded due to lack of a DNA match.

Whether the actual percentage is closer to two or fifteen, this means that each year, thousands, or tens of thousands, of innocent Americans are branded as criminals and sent to prison for an offense they did not commit. Innocence Project co-founder, Peter Neufeld laments, "the number of people who are unjustly convicted in our system is extraordinarily high."

TYPES AND CAUSES

For years, Americans assumed prosecutors were acting in a fair and honest manner. But in the late 1990s, the received wisdom came under challenge when the *Pittsburgh Post-Gazette* and *Chicago Tribune* ran separate exposés revealing widespread prosecutorial impropriety, which is defined in this White Paper as "misconduct by the relevant Rules of Ethical Conduct," violation of any law, or other conduct that prejudices the administration of justice, whether intentional or inadvertent, exonerated following DNA analysis, witness recantation, confession by the actual offender, or by other means.

The year 2007 turned out to be a watershed as Americans were riveted by events in the Duke University lacrosse case, eventually resulting in the North Carolina State Bar's decision to disbar District Attorney Michael Nifong for "dishonesty, fraud, deceit and misrepresentation."

Culture of Prosecutorial Infallibility

Prosecutors are subjected to a variety of powerful incentives that serve to reward zealous advocacy: the gratitude of victims, favorable media coverage, career promotions, appointment to judgeships, and the allure of high political office. The most insidious incentive of all may be a culture of prosecutorial infallibility. This mindset gives rise to practices that can only be termed bizarre, such as prosecutors who reportedly wear neckties decorated with images of nooses or who throw a party after "winning" a death sentence.

One prosecutor inquired of candidates for employment if previous experiences in the law had provided them with a chance to, "taste blood." The prosecutor revealed he only intended to hire trial lawyers who had already, "tasted blood," and liked it.

In Louisiana, ADA James Williams once admitted, "There was no thrill for me unless there was a chance for the death penalty." Williams reputedly kept a miniature electric chair on his desk, wired to a battery to deliver a jolt to anyone who might doubt his intentions.

EXTENT OF MISCONDUCT

No one knows the exact extent of prosecutor misconduct. That's because many prosecutorial activities take place behind closed doors, rendering any misconduct difficult to detect. An inkling of the problem comes from the National Registry of

Exonerations, which concluded 43% of wrongful convictions are attributable to official misconduct. Legal experts have long painted a picture of secrecy, tactical short-cuts, even arrogance itself. The most telling critiques come from former prosecutors:

- Joseph F. Lawless, author of a standard reference book on prosecutor ethics, wrote, "The concept of fairness, once thought to be fundamental in a free society, is generally no longer found in the prosecutor's office".

- Ohio attorney general Jim Petro has noted, "While innocent human error can lead to wrongful convictions, we also now know that many abuses, misrepresentations, and improper tactics are often involved."

- Former New York City Assistant District Attorney Bennett Gersham worries the problem may be worsening: "The last 15 years are most notable for a vast accretion of power by prosecutors, increased deference by courts to prosecutorial prerogatives, and a general failure of courts and disciplinary bodies to impose meaningful sanctions on prosecutors for misconduct."

Other legal experts offer similar perspectives:

- Harvard law professor Alan Dershowitz has opined that prosecutorial misconduct is "rampant.

- American University professor AJ Davis refers to the problem as "pervasive."

- Regarding the unethical practice of over-charging, California defense attorney Benjamin Theule alleges the practice is now "common."

- Civil rights attorney Harvey Silverglate believes over-charging has reached the point of becoming, "ingrained," into the process.

- In Texas, defense attorney John Floyd asserts, "Prosecutorial misconduct has been endemic in the state's criminal justice system over the past five decades."

The public is awakening to the existence of the problem, as well. According to a 2013 national survey.

- 42.8% of respondents say prosecutor misconduct is widespread.
- 71.8% believe new laws are needed to curb prosecutor misconduct.

Reaching the Highest Levels

Prosecutor misconduct extends to the highest levels; indeed, the ethical state of affairs may be even more dire.

National District Attorneys Association

The National District Attorneys Association (NDAA) is the trade organization that represents the nearly 30,000 prosecutor's and district attorney's around the country. When it comes to proactively addressing the problem, the group is steadfastly non-committal. A search of the NDAA website using the search terms "prosecutorial misconduct" or "prosecutorial error" fails to identify a single office, program, or even publication that is devoted to rectifying this problem.

Some NDAA officials are working to narrow the scope of the definition of prosecutor misconduct to encompass "conduct that was known by a prosecutor to be improper and prejudicial but that the prosecutor nevertheless pursued with the intent to affect the outcome of the case." Of course, establishing prior knowledge and intent is an exceedingly difficult standard to meet. Relying upon this narrow definition, the National District Attorneys Association has concluded that prosecutorial misconduct is, "exceedingly rare." Indeed, the NDAA passed a resolution in 2010 admonishing judges who decide to use the phrase, "prosecutorial misconduct" in its broader and more widely used sense.

John Floyd & Billy Sinclair, Fairness in Disclosure of Evidence Act seeks to address Growing

Concern over Prosecutorial Misconduct and Wrongful Convictions, John T. Floyd Law Firm (July 18, 2012).

Even when it comes to upholding the legal principle of equal treatment under law, the Association falls short. The NDAA sponsors a National Center for the Prosecution of Violence Against *Women*, but offers no parallel program regarding violence against *men*. This programmatic imbalance may have contributed to the fact that males have been found to be "consistently treated more severely at every stage of the prosecution process."

Department of Justice

The U.S. Department of Justice has been implicated in the problem, as well. Attorney Harvey Silverglate stresses the fact that, "too many ordinary, well-meaning, and innocent people get caught in the maw of the Department of Justice's prosecutorial machinery." Former U.S. Attorney Joseph Digenova has revealed, "the Department [of

Justice] is in real trouble. This is serious business. These career prosecutors believe that nobody can touch them. Nobody!

The problem can be traced back to the early 1990s when the U.S. Department of Justice asserted its prosecutors were not bound by the ethical codes of the states in which cases were prosecuted. The stalemate was not resolved until 1999 when Congress passed the Federal Prosecutor Ethics Act. But requiring prosecutors to abide by state ethical codes did not eliminate the Department's ethical woes. In 2009 a federal judge set aside the conviction of former Senator Ted Stevens of Alaska. Announcing his decision, Judge Emmett Sullivan took the prosecutors involved in the case to the ethical woodshed: "In nearly 25 years on the bench, I've never seen anything approaching the mishandling and misconduct that I've seen in this case."

Ethical lapses continue to the present time. When internet activist Aaron Swartz illegally downloaded computer files, Department of Justice prosecutors filed 13 charges that carried the possibility of 35 years behind bars and up to a $1 million fine. Prosecutors then offered Swartz a deal to plead guilty to all charges and spend six months in jail.

CONSEQUENCES OF MISCONDUCT

Mistakes can happen. But if you don't do anything to stop them from happening again, you can't keep calling them mistakes.

A number of ethical standards govern the practices of the prosecutorial profession. Most influential is the ABA Model Rule 3.8, Special Responsibilities of a Prosecutor which is presented in Appendix A of this White Paper. The ABA Model Rule 3.8 establishes the criteria by which to evaluate allegations of prosecutor misconduct, and has been implemented either verbatim or with minor modifications in virtually every state in the country.

Other relevant ethical standards include:

1. ABA Standards for Criminal Justice "The Prosecution Function" supplements the Model Rules.The prosecutorial Standards address General Standards, Organization of the Prosecution Function, investigation for Prosecution Decision, Plea Discussions, Trial, and Sentencing.

2. The United States Attorneys' Manual is an internal handbook which provides general policies and procedures relevant to the work of U.S. Attorneys' offices.

3. The National Prosecution Standards, developed by the National District Attorneys Association, are crafted as a detailed, yet purely aspirational guide.

A review of these standards reveals they are broad in scope and detailed in their exposition. So the problem cannot be blamed on a lack of ethical guidance so what happens when ethical codes are violated? Nine studies have analyzed the professional consequences of prosecutor misconduct. Collectively, these studies examined prosecutorial misconduct conducted at the both state and national levels from 1963 – 2013. Of the 3,625 instances of misconduct identified, these studies reveal that public sanctions are imposed in only 63 cases -- less than 2% of the time (Appendix B).

Often these sanctions represented only a proverbial "slap-of-the-wrist." For example in the nearly 50 cases identified in the Center for Public Integrity analysis, the most common sanction was to assess the prosecutor with the costs of the disciplinary hearings, occurring in 24 cases. In only 14 instances was a prosecutor suspended or disbarred from practice.

Indeed, when a prosecutor violates ethical precepts, judges and appellate courts seemingly bend over backwards to excuse the conduct. Even in the most reprehensible cases, judges typically do not refer the case for disciplinary action and ethics boards fail to apply sanctions. Courts rely upon fault-absolving notions like, "harmless error," a doctrine that has been termed the, "lie that the criminal justice system tells itself."

Reflecting on the current state of affairs, former ADA Robin Barton has bemoaned the, "lack of outrage by other prosecutors, who should be condemning this conduct and calling for reforms to prevent similar behavior."

TAXPAYER BURDEN

No one knows how much money is misspent each year as a result of prosecutor misconduct. This can involve an appeal, an appellate reversal, a retrial, investigational efforts to trace the real offender, possible civil lawsuits, and compensatory payments – as well as the emotional costs to victims who are forced to relive the tragedy.

In Texas, 45 wrongful convictions were estimated to cost taxpayers $8.6 million. One analysis of 85 exonerations in Illinois found the wrongful convictions had imprisoned innocent people for 926 years and cost $214 million.

Housing Costs

The costs to house wrongfully convicted inmates can be staggering, as well. A Department of Justice-funded study of post-rape conviction DNA analyses in Virginia found in 15% of convictions, the DNA of the prisoner and perpetrator did not match.

Nationwide, 160,800 prisoners who were convicted for rape or other sexual assault are currently under state jurisdiction. Extrapolating the Virginia false conviction figure to a national sample, we conclude that 24,120 current inmates were wrongfully convicted and imprisoned.

The average state corrections expenditure per inmate is $28,323. This translates into an annual expenditure of $683 million. This is an underestimate because the number does not include defendants wrongfully detained in local jails or in military or federal prisons, as well as the many detained persons who are still awaiting trial.

ONE IN ONE HUNDRED

If we were to identify a single riveting fact that encapsulates the excess of our current criminal justice system, it would be this:

160,800 prisoners x 0.15 false conviction rate = 24,100 prisoners wrongly convicted. Nearly one in 100 adult Americans is currently serving time behind bars, by far the largest proportion of any nation in the world. By comparison, the United States has six times as many prisoners as Canada or China, even after total population is taken into account.

This deplorable state of affairs is the product of many factors. Lawmakers have passed too many laws with poorly-defined offenses. Law enforcement officials have made too many arrests that lack probable cause. The Supreme Court has failed to uphold appellate decisions of official wrong-doing. But as the most powerful stakeholder in the criminal justice system, the prosecutorial profession must shoulder a major portion of the responsibility, and work proactively to remedy the abuses.

Each year, thousands of Americans are victimized by prosecutors who overcharge, withhold key evidence, and engage in a myriad of other forms of professional misconduct. When these persons later seek redress, they encounter denial, resistance, and delays. More often than not, their efforts to receive even an apology end in futile exasperation.

Fundamental reform is long over-due, and corrective policies have been delineated. Prosecutors, lawmakers, concerned citizens, and others need to take action to restore the luster to Lady Justice.

JOSEPH WILTZ

ANALYSES OF PUBLIC SANCTIONS FOR PROSECUTORIAL MISCONDUCT

Scope	Criteria	Year	#of Cases of Misconduct	# of Public Sanctions
United States	Homicide cases in which appellate courts reversed a conviction due to prosecutor misconduct	1963 - 1999	389	0
United States	Cases in which prosecutor misconduct affected the fairness of pending criminal proceedings or infringed on the constitutional rights of defendants	1970 - 2003	2,012	Fewer than 50
United States	Cases in which judges determined that federal prosecutors	1997 - 2010	201	1

86 | P a g e

	violated laws or ethics rules			
Arizona	Appellate court findings of prosecutoria l misconduct	2004 - 2008	20	0
Arizona	Death-penalty cases reviewed by the Arizona Supreme Court	2002 - 2013	16	2
California	State and federal appellate rulings of prosecutoria l misconduct	1997 - 2011	707	6
New York	Trial and appellate court findings of prosecutoria l misconduct	2004 - 2008	151	3
Pennsylv ania	Appellate court findings of prosecutoria l misconduct	2004 - 2008	46	0

Texas	Trial and Appellate Court Findings of Prosecutorial Misconduct	2004 - 2008	91	1
	TOTAL		3,625	63

CHAPTER 11

THE EPIDEMIC OF BLACKS BEING KILLED, ARRESTED, MISTREATED BY POLICE

According to information published by the FBI, there is data which shows there have been 400 "justifiable homicide" cases by Law Enforcement Officers each year. Researchers analyzed police public contact survey (PPCS) data and Bureau Of Justice statistics survey of inmates in local jails data and concluded that 1.7% of all contacts result in police threats or use of force, while 20% of arrests do.

A widely publicized report in October 2014 by Pro Publica, a leading investigative and data Journalism outlet, concluded that young black males are 21 times likely to be shot by police than their white counterparts; the 1,217 deadly police shootings from 2010 to 2012 captured in the Federal data show that blacks ages 15 to 19, were killed at a rate of 31.17 per million, while Just 1.47 per million white males in that age range died at the hands of police.

A whopping 99% of police brutality complaints go uninvestigated. If one had the opportunity to review the records of all police departments nationwide, I am sure that we would all agree that we would be astounded over the amount of complaints that have been filed by citizens, alleging brutality, bias, and civil rights violation, that were never investigated. What is so ironic, is that majority of the crimes committed by police, are against blacks. Should we have to continue wondering why there is a lack of investigative actions taken against police officers?

A report from the CDC in Oklahoma stated that the rate at which black people are killed per capita by Law enforcement is greater than anywhere else in the country or nationwide.

CHAPTER 12

POLICE MISCONDUCT

The National Police Misconduct statistics and Reporting Project (NPMSRP) reported the 2010 statistics and reporting project recorded 4,861 reports of Police misconduct that involved 6,613 sworn Law enforcement Officers. 354 were agency leaders such as Chiefs and Sheriff's. Of the 6,613 officers involved in reported allegations, 1,575 were for excessive force, followed by sexual misconduct complaints at 9.3 %, then theft, fraud, robbery 7.2%. 618 officers were involved in sexual misconduct complaints.

CONCLUSION

As mentioned in the beginning, this book dealt with the mental and physical trauma that black Americans endure by the hands of the oppressors that inflicts injustice, racism, white supremacy and deceitfulness. So often, people make comments such as, "When is he or she going to change? He or she cannot stay out of jail...they never learn."

My prayer is that the information provided in this book would not only enlighten those who read it, but also help to explain the mental state of those who have been incarcerated. Many of the atrocities that occurred during slavery, which did tremendous psychological and economic damage to African Americans, are similar to the same processes used to enslave African Americans today in the prison industrial complex.

To make this point more clearly, the 13th Amendment of the United States Constitution says that slavery is allowed to this day if a person has been convicted of a felony. Similar to the Fugitive

Slave Acts, this implies that any African-American who has a label placed on their head due to an arbitrary law (such as the crack-to-powder disparity) can then be made into a slave. So, when someone says that prison is modern day slavery, they aren't exaggerating. The Constitution says that it is.

When we understand the methodologies used by Willie Lynch, to control the minds of enslaved Africans, no doubt, we will understand that it is the same methodology that is used today to control the minds of Black Americans, educated or uneducated. We will have a broader understanding of the mental struggle of those who have been incarcerated for long periods of time.

Due to the fact that 85% of the Black population are unconsciously unaware that their actions are still rooted in yesterday's slavery, most blacks who are in political and judicial positions either turn the blind eye, afraid, or just plain ignorant to what is happening to Black Americans. It is a disgraceful thing not only to the Black race, but unto God for anyone to treat human beings this way because of color, or better yet because of hidden fear that the oppressor struggles with. It is even more disgraceful for the Black Americans who God has placed in political or judicial positions, to allow unjust, and bias laws to directly affect blacks and the poor. If you are a Law maker, a Judge, etc. and you are either ignore or take part in the unjust and bias laws that are passed, you are just as guilty.

God's word says in Proverbs 10:1 (NLT), *Destruction is certain for the unjust Judges, for those who issue unfair Laws.* Proverbs 22:7 (NLT) says, *Those who plant seeds of injustice will harvest disaster. And their reign of terror will end.* Proverbs 22:22 (NLT) *Do not rob the poor because they are poor or exploit the needy in court. For the Lord is their defender, he will injure anyone who injures them.*

The "Willie Lynch" methodology of mind manipulation is so prevalent in the world today that black leaders are overly cautious and fearful when it comes to talking about race issues in America. Manipulation says, when Blacks talk about or highlight acts of racism, they are accused of being racist, or creating division. When anyone becomes fearful of man rather than God, they are selling their souls to Satan. Their motive doesn't matter whether it was an attempt to accomplish their selfish desires, or fear of retaliation,

When you become too afraid to tell the truth and take a stand for righteousness, you have made the person(s) you fear your God. According to the New Living Translation Bible, *You must not bow down to them or worship them, for I, the Lord your God, am a jealous God who will not tolerate your affection for any other Gods.*

Never believe that slavery is disconnected from the present. It wasn't that long ago. If you take the age of your parents and multiply it by three (or four), you are probably somewhere near the slave era. This is just a few generations back.

My suggestion is that a reform of the criminal Justice system is a vital necessity. The reform should consist of:

- Giving Judges a more active role
- Restricting voir dire
- Selecting jurors with expertise
- Allowing jurors to ask limited questions
- Discipline court officials who err
- Form independent organization to monitor the conduct of court officials and police
- Remove or change immunity laws

ABOUT THE AUTHOR

Joseph Wiltz is currently the president, founder , and Spiritual motivational speaker of Greatness IN Me, INC. Joseph was inspired to start this organization from his first-hand experience of the physical and mental abuse that people who are incarcerated go through, as well as the mental trauma that he see's other people experience from the system of racism, discrimination, inequality, and injustice. Through years of spiritual training, being a police officer, a prison guard at one of the second largest penitentiaries in Louisiana, and former owner of a private investigation business, Joseph was able to hear and see people's hurts and pains.

While working in the prison system, he had the opportunity to speak to murderers, arm robbers, rapists, and more. These experiences caused him to develop a heart of compassion for the hurting and the lost. Mr. Wiltz has had the opportunity to counsel many hurting people from all walks of life through the church in which he attended.

Mr. Wiltz is married to Donna Wiltz, the owner of a salon and Day Spa. Together they have raised two beautiful sons, and three beautiful daughters.

Organization: Greatness in me

Website: www.greatnessinme.com

Email: jwiltz.greatnessinme@yahoo.com

Phone No.: (225) 284-6929

www.ingramcontent.com/pod-product-compliance
Lightning Source LLC
Chambersburg PA
CBHW070830180526
45168CB00002B/787